Devotions & Prayers of CHARLES H. SPURGEON

52 devotions, each combined with a selected prayer

Donald E. Demaray, Editor

Spurgeon, C

BAKER BOOK HOUSE
Grand Rapids, Michigan

242
S772

Copyright 1960 by
Baker Book House Company

Library of Congress
Catalog Card Number:
60-9581

Paperback edition issued
September 1976

ISBN: 0-8010-2866-3

PHOTOLITHOPRINTED BY CUSHING - MALLOY, INC.
ANN ARBOR, MICHIGAN, UNITED STATES OF AMERICA
1976

For

My Mother

GRACE VORE DEMARAY

PREFACE

"Read, above all things, your Bible," said W. Robertson Nicoll, "and whatever books you add to your Bible, add some volumes of your great apostle Charles H. Spurgeon . . . ." Good advice indeed! especially when it comes to devotional literature, for Mr. Spurgeon was a master at pictorializing the best in meditative thought. Spurgeon found himself living with God's Word and its interpreters. Anything and everything that made God clear to the heart was relevant to Charles Spurgeon. No doubt it was this continuous soaking in the things of God that made him such a remarkable devotional writer.

The Spurgeon success-story is well known. He began to preach at only sixteen years of age and published perhaps more sermons than any preacher in church history. He published enough materials, sermonic and otherwise, to fill a good-sized encyclopedia.* Enormous crowds came to hear Spurgeon; they came quite literally by the thousands. Sometimes he preached to as many as 23,000 in one sitting and Arthur T. Pierson once estimated that Spurgeon preached to at least 10,000,000 people during the course of his thirty-four years of professional ministry.

Spurgeon's works were translated into numerous languages, including Arabic, Armenian, Chinese, Congo, Danish, Dutch, Estonian, Gaelic, German, Spanish, Norwegian, Polish, Russian, Swedish. In addition there were translations for the blind in Braille.

---

*" . . . The sheer bulk of the literary productions of Charles Spurgeon are equal to twenty-seven volumes of the ninth edition of Encyclopedia Britanica."—Wilbur M. Smith in *The Treasury of Charles H. Spurgeon* (Fleming H. Revell Company, 1955), p. 12.

But Spurgeon would not have us look at the gigantic output of his work so much as at the God of his work—the God who can meet the real needs of real human beings. He would have us spend time with God at the outset of every day in order to see things in righteous perspective and to get rightly orientated for the day's work. Spurgeon would have us find peace of mind and composure of heart. He is saying in every one of these devotional selections that God is, and that He is the rewarder of them that diligently seek Him; that there is actually a solution to the everyday frustrations, the little irritations that come along, and that this solution is discovered in God Himself.

* * * * *

These prayers and devotions have been taken from the sermons, journal, letters, notebooks, autobiography, and other writings of Charles H. Spurgeon. Where the language patterns have seemed out of date, the editor and compiler has taken the liberty of making changes, but in no instance has the meaning been altered.

For the kind co-operation of the Baker Book House staff, especially Mr. Herman Baker, founder and owner of the House, I wish to express my gratitude. I wish also to express special appreciation to Mr. Cornelius Zylstra, editor for Baker Book House, who has been a never-failing source of encouragement throughout the course of this project, as well as at many another time. To the Seattle Pacific College librarians, Miss Margaret A. Bursell and Mrs. Mary B. Dade, I wish to extend further thanks for assistance in locating Spurgeon materials. To my secretary, Miss Elizabeth Leise, goes praise for a job well done.

Donald E. Demaray

Seattle Pacific College

" . . . *The way to spiritual health is to exercise one's self in holy contemplation.*"

—Charles Haddon Spurgeon

A Challenge to Young Men

1

Remember now thy Creator in the days of thy youth, while the evil days come not, nor the years draw nigh, when thou shalt say, I have no pleasure in them. — *Ecclesiastes* 12:1

I DO not believe that any age was better than this, all things considered, but this is the time when we shall want our young men to be strong.... Battles are coming in which they will need to stand with firm foot. There will be strifes in which they will not be of the slightest value if they cannot brave the conflict. Rest assured these are not silken days, nor times to make us dream that we have won the victory. Our fathers, where are they? They are looking down upon us from their thrones, but what do they see? Do they see us wearing the crown and waving the palm-branch? If so, they see us lunatics indeed, for that were a madman's sport; but rather they see us sharpening our swords afresh, and buckling on our panoply anew, to fight the same fight which they fought under other circumstances. The young blood of the church, under God, is our great hope in the conflict of King Jesus. The young men of the church must be in the next twenty years the very soul and vigor of it, and, therefore, may God raise up among us a goodly seed, a race of heroes, swifter than eagles for zeal, and stronger than lions for faith.

Prayer

Lord, I pray Thee, open the young men's eyes, that they may see. . . . And O Lord, gird them for the fight, and make them to be among those who overcome through the blood of the Lamb and through the word of their testimony, because they "love not their lives unto the death." Amen.

Praying Saves Time

But seek ye first the kingdom of God, and his righteousness; and all these things shall be added unto you. — Matthew 6:33

2

SOMETIMES we think we are too busy to pray. That is a great mistake, for praying is a saving of time. You remember Luther's remark, "I have so much to do today that I shall never get through it with less than three hours prayer." If we have no time to pray we must make time, for if God has given us time for secondary duties, he must have given us time for primary ones; and to draw near to him is a primary duty, and we must let nothing set it to one side. There is no real need to sacrifice any duty; we have time enough for all, if we are not idle; and indeed, the one will help the other instead of clashing with it. When Edward Payson was a student at college, he found he had so much to do to attend his classes and prepare for examinations, that he could not spend as much time as he should in private prayer; but at last, waking up to the feeling that he was going back in divine things through his habits, he took due time for devotion; and he asserts in his diary that he did more in his studies in a single week after he had spent time with God in prayer, than he had accomplished in twelve months before.

Prayer

O GOD, multiply our ability to make use of time. Strengthen within us the conviction that if we give the Lord his due, we shall indeed have enough for all necessary purposes. In this matter, as in others, teach us to act upon the command to seek first the kingdom of God and his righteousness, for all "these things shall be added" to us. Amen.

The Science of Charity

And this is his commandment, That we should believe on the name of his Son Jesus Christ, and love one another, as he gave us commandment. — I John 3:23

3

WHEN [St.] Bernard chanced to espy a poor man meanly apparelled, he would say to himself: 'Truly, Bernard, this man hath more patience beneath his cross than thou hast.' But if he saw a rich man delicately clothed, then he would say: 'It may be that this man, under his delicate clothing, hath a better soul than thou hast under thy religious habit!' "

This showed an excellent charity! Oh, that we could learn it! It is easy to think evil of all men, for there is sure to be some fault about each one which even the least discerning may readily discover; but it is far more worthy of a Christian, and shows much more nobility of soul, to spy out the good in each fellow believer. This needs a larger mind as well as a better heart, and hence it should be a point of honor to practice ourselves in it till we obtain an aptitude for it. Any simpleton might be set to sniff out offensive odors; but it would require a scientific man to bring to us all the fragrant essences and rare perfumes which lie hid in field and garden. Oh, to learn the science of Christian charity!

Prayer

O GOD, teach us the art of charity, far more to be esteemed than the most lucrative of human labors. Show us that love is the true alchemy, for charity towards others, abundantly practiced, would be the death of envy and the life of fellowship, the overthrow of self and the enthronement of Thy divine grace. Amen.

The Preeminence of Christ

4

And he is the head of the body, the church: who is the beginning, the firsborn from the dead; that in all things he might have the preeminence. — *Colossians 1:18*

As you grow in grace you will find that many doctrines and points of church government which once appeared to you to be all-important, though you will still value them, will seem but of small consequence compared with Christ himself. Like the traveller ascending the Alps to reach the summit of Mont Blanc, at first he observes that lord of the hills as one horn among many, and often in the twistings of his upward path he sees other peaks which appear more elevated than that monarch of mountains; but when at last he is near the summit, he sees all the rest of the hills beneath his feet, and like a mighty wedge of alabaster, Mont Blanc pierces the very clouds. So, as we grow in grace, other things sink and Jesus rises. They must decrease, but Christ must increase; until he alone fills the full horizon of your soul, and rises clear and bright and glorious up into the very heaven of God.

Prayer

O LORD, we beseech Thee mold us into Thine own image. Let us live in Thee and live like Thee. Let us gaze upon Thy glory till we are transformed by the sight and become Christ-like among the sons of men. Amen.

To Will One Thing

5

The light of the body is the eye: therefore when thine eye is single, thy whole body also is full of light; but when thine eye is evil, thy body also is full of darkness. — *Luke 11:34*

THAT eminent ornithologist, M. Audubon, who produced accurate drawings and descriptions of all the birds of the American Continent, made the perfection of that work the one object of his life. In order to achieve this he had to earn his own living by painting portraits, and by other labours; he had to traverse frozen seas, forests, jungles, prairies, mountains, swollen rivers. He exposed himself to perils of every sort. Now, whatever Audubon was doing, he was fighting his way towards his one object, the production of his history of American birds. Whether he was painting a lady's portrait, paddling a canoe, shooting a raccoon, or felling a tree, his one aim was a bird book. He had said to himself, "I mean to carve my name amongst the naturalists as having produced a complete ornithological work for America," and this resolution ate him up, and subdued his whole life. He accomplished his work because he gave himself wholly to it. This is the way in which the Christian man should make Christ his element. All that he does should be subservient to this one thing, "That I may finish my course with joy, that I may deliver my testimony for Christ, that I may glorify God whether I live or die."

16

Prayer

LORD Jesus, take from us now everything that would hinder the closest communion with God. Remove any wish or
desire that might hamper us, we pray
Thee. Any memory of either sorrow or
care that might hinder the fixing of our
affection wholly on our God, take it away
now. Amen.

The Utmost Stretch of Manhood

6

And he said to them all, If any man will come after me, let him deny himself, and take up his cross daily, and follow me. — Luke 9:23

IF you could know the regrets at the end of your life, would not these be the regrets, that you have not served Christ better, loved him more, spoken of him oftener, given more generously to his cause, and more uniformly proved yourself to be consecrated to him? I am afraid that such would be the form of the regrets of Paradise, if any could intrude within those gates of pearl. Come, let us live while we live! Let us live up to the utmost stretch of our manhood! Let us ask the Lord to brace our nerves and make us true crusaders, knights of the blood-red cross, consecrated men and women, who, for the love we bear Christ's name, will count labor to be ease, and suffering to be joy, and reproach to be honor, and loss to be gain! If we have never yet given ourselves wholly up to Christ as his disciples, now hard by his cross, where we see his wounds still bleeding afresh, and himself quivering in pain for us, let us pledge ourselves in his strength, that we give ourselves wholly to him without reserve, and so may he help us by his Spirit, that the vow may be redeemed and the resolve may be carried out, that we may love Christ, and dying may find it gain.

Prayer

LORD, we want to live while we live. We do pray that we may not merely groan out an existence here below, nor live as earthworms crawling back into our holes; but, oh! give us to live as we ought to live, with a new life that Thou hast put into us, with the divine quickening which has lifted us as much above common men as men are lifted above the beasts that perish. Amen.

The Spirit of God

7

And Pharaoh said unto his servants, Can we find such a one as this is, a man in whom the Spirit of God is? — *Genesis 41:38*

Without the Spirit of God, we are like a ship stranded on the beach; when the tide has receded, there is no moving her until the flood shall once again lift her from the sands. We are like a frozen ship frostbound in the far-off Arctic Sea: until the Spirit of God shall thaw the chilly coldness of our natural estate, and bid the life-floods of our heart flow forth, there we must lie, cold, cheerless, lifeless, powerless. The Christian, like the mariner, depends upon the breath of heaven, or his ship is without motion. We are like the plants of the field: all the winter through vegetation sleeps wrapped up in her frost garments, but when the mysterious influence of spring is felt, she unbinds her cloak to put on her vest of many colors, while every bud begins to swell and each flower to open. And so a church lies asleep in a long and dreary winter until God the Holy Spirit looses the bands of lethargy, and hearts bud and blossom, and the time of the singing of birds is come.

Prayer

LORD sanctify us. Oh! that Thy spirit might come and saturate every faculty, subdue every passion, and use every power of our nature for obedience to God. Come, Holy Spirit, we do know Thee; Thou hast often overshadowed us. Come, more fully take possession of us. Amen.

Face Up to Your Problems with God

8   If we say that we have no sin, we deceive
ourselves, and the truth is not in us. —
I John 1:8

HE is an imposter who strives to make
men forget their spiritual sorrows instead
of leading them to the true cure. This is
like a man in debt, who drinks to drown
his thoughts; but this neither pays the
debt nor postpones the reckoning."

When conscience is uneasy, it is foolish
as well as wicked to attempt to smother
its cries with worldly merriment. Nay, let
us hear it patiently. If we be in debt let
us know it, and set about meeting our
liabilities like honest men; but to burn
the ledger and discharge the clerk is a
madman's way of going to work. O soul,
be true to thyself. Face thine own case,
however bad it may be; for refusing to
know and consider the sure facts will not
alter or improve them. He is a cruel doc-
tor who tells the afflicted patient that he
ails nothing, and thus sets him for the
time at his ease, at the terrible cost of
future disease, rendered incurable by delay.

Prayer

LORD, bring me to the bar of my conscience now, lest I stand condemned at thy bar of judgment hereafter.

Come near, our Father, come very near to Thy children. Some of us are weak in body and faint in heart. Soon, O God, lay Thy right hand upon us and say unto us, "Fear not." Amen.

Seek Ye the Lord

9

Seek ye the Lord while he may be found, call ye upon him while he is near: Let the wicked forsake his way, and the unrighteous man his thoughts; and let him return unto the Lord, and he will have mercy upon him; and to our God, for he will abundantly pardon. — Isaiah 55:6-7

THERE have been some men in this world who have had little else to recommend them except that by which they have attracted their fellow men to yield them homage — like Napoleon Bonaparte, for instance, when he said to his soldiers at Austerlitz, "Soldiers, this battle must be a thunder-clap; we must hear no more of the foe." And the men, filled with eagerness by his passionate energy, did his bidding, and made it such a thunder-clap that all Europe shook beneath the march of those men-at-arms. He had the power, somehow or other, of making men yield to him, as if they were all machines, impelled by the force of his personal will. They were not dragged into battle, but rushed with enthusiasm to the fight, longing to win glory or death. Now, the voice of God should be to the Christian a voice that speaks to all his soul, wakes up his dormant faculties, and stirs the enthusiasm of his noblest nature, so that his heart says, "I will indeed seek thy face." As the British sailor, when Nelson said to him, "Ready?" replied, "Ready, ay, ready," and fired red-hot shot at the foe, so should our hearts respond to God, "Seek ye my face."

Prayer

LORD, blessed be Thy name for telling
me to seek Thy face, for Thou and I art
of one mind; Thou lovest me to seek Thy
face, and I love to seek Thee; my heart
responds — not my lips, not my body,
dragged slavishly into the form of obedience — but my heart says, "Thy face, Lord,
will I seek." Amen.

Why Dread the Clouds?

10   ... He had commanded the clouds from above, and opened the doors of heaven. — *Psalm 78:23*

WHY, then, do we dread the clouds which now darken our sky? True, for a while they hide the sun, but the sun is not quenched; it will be out again before long. Meanwhile those black clouds are filled with rain; and the blacker they are, the most likely they will yield plentiful showers.

How can we have rain without clouds? Our troubles have always brought us blessings, and they always will. They are the dark chariots of bright grace. These clouds will empty themselves before long, and every tender herb will be gladder for the shower. Our God may drench us with grief, but He will refresh us with mercy. Our Lord's love letters often come to us in black-edged envelopes. His wagons rumble, but they are loaded with benefits. His rod blossoms with sweet flowers and nourishing fruits. Let us not worry about the clouds, but sing because May flowers are brought to us through the April clouds and showers.

Prayer

O LORD, the clouds are the dust of Thy feet! How near Thou art in the cloudy and dark day! Love beholds Thee, and is glad. Faith sees the clouds emptying themselves and making the little hills rejoice on every side. Amen.

Come As You Are

Come unto me, all ye that labour and are heavy laden, and I will give you rest. — Matthew 11:28

A CERTAIN king was accustomed on set occasions to entertain all the beggars of the city. Around him sat his courtiers, all clothed in rich apparel; the beggars sat at the same table in their rags of poverty. Now, it came to pass that on a certain day one of the courtiers had spoiled his silken apparel so that he dare not put it on, and he said to himself, "I cannot go to the king's feast today, for my robe is not presentable." He sat weeping, till the thought struck him, "Tomorrow, when the king holds his feast, some will come as courtiers, happily decked in their beautiful array; but others will come and be made quite as welcome who will be dressed in rags. So long as I may see the king's face and sit at the king's table, I will enter with the beggars." So it was that without mourning he put on the rags of a beggar, and he saw the king's face as well as if he had worn his scarlet linen.

My soul has done this on many an occasion and I bid you do the same; if you cannot come as a saint, come as a sinner, only do come, and you shall receive joy and peace.

Prayer

O THOU who art King of kings and
Lord of lords, we worship Thee.

> Before Jehovah's awful throne
> We bow with sacred joy.

We can truly say that we delight in God.
O Lord, we desire to find Thee. Our longing is to feel Thy presence. The furnace
of affliction grows cool when Thou art
there, and the house of prayer when Thou
art present is none other than the house
of God, and it is the very gate of heaven.
Amen.

The God Who Cares and Aids

12 Casting all your care upon him; for he careth for you. — *I Peter 5:7*

WHEN the flock is on the march, it will happen, unless the shepherd is very watchful, that the lambs will lag behind. Those great Syrian flocks which feed in the plains of Palestine have to be driven many miles, because the pasturage is scant and the flocks are numerous; and in long journeys the lambs drop one by one for weariness, and then the shepherd carries them. So it is in the progress of the great Christian church; persecuted often, always more or less molested by the outside world, there are some who flag; they cannot keep up the pace; the spiritual warfare is too severe for them. They love their Lord; they would if they could be amongst the foremost; but, through the cares of this world, through weakness of mind, through a lack of spiritual vigor, they become lame and are ready to perish; such faint hearts are the peculiar care of their tender Lord.

Prayer

GREAT Father, be with Thy waiting people; any in great trouble do Thou greatly help; any that are despondent do Thou comfort and cheer; any that have erred and are smarting under their own sin, do Thou bring back and heal their wounds; any that this day are panting after holiness do Thou give them the desire of their hearts; any that are longing for usefulness do Thou lead them into ways of usefulness. Amen.

Men Ought Always to Pray

13

And he spake a parable unto them to this end, that men ought always to pray, and not to faint. — *Luke 18:1*

OUR Lord meant by saying men ought always to pray, that **they ought to be always in the spirit of prayer,** always ready to pray — like the old knights always wearing their weapons where they could readily reach them, and always ready to encounter wounds or death for the sake of the cause which they championed. Those grim warriors often slept in their armor; so even when we sleep we are still to be in the spirit of prayer, so that if perchance we wake in the night we may still be with God. Our soul, having received the divine centripetal influence which makes it seek its heavenly center, should be evermore naturally rising towards God himself. Our heart is to be like those beacons and watchtowers which were prepared along the coast of England when the invasion of the Armada was hourly expected, not always blazing, but with the wood always dry, and the match always there, the whole pile being ready to blaze up at the appointed moment. Our souls should be in such a condition that ejaculatory prayer should be frequent. No need to pause in business and fall down upon the knees; the spirit should send up its silent, short, swift petition to the throne of grace.

Prayer

WE do bless Thee, O Lord, for instituting the blessed ordinance of prayer. What could we do without it, and we take great shame to ourselves that we should use it so little. We pray that we may be men of prayer, taken up with it, that it may take us up and bear us as on its wings towards heaven. Amen.

Trust God

. . . I have put my trust in the Lord God, that I may declare all thy works. — Psalm 73:28

THAT is a grand story of Alexander's confidence in his friend and physician. When the physician had mixed him a potion for his sickness, a letter was put into Alexander's hand, warning him not to drink the medicine, for it was poisoned. He held the letter in one hand and the cup in the other, and in the presence of his friend and physician, he drank the contents, and after he had drained the cup, he bade his friend look at the letter, and judge of his confidence in him. Alexander had unstaggering faith in his friend. "See now," said he, "how I have trusted you." This is the assurance which the believer should exercise towards his God. The cup is very bitter, and some tell us it will prove to be deadly. Unbelief whispers in our ear, "Your coming tribulation will utterly crush you." Drink it, my friend, and say, "If he slay me, yet will I trust in him." It cannot be that God should be unfaithful to his promise, or unmindful of his covenant. Your trial, then, will cease when it culminates: he will make darkness light before you when the darkest hour of the night has struck.

Prayer

MAKE me Thy faithful servant, O my God; may I honor Thee in my day and generation, and be consecrated forever to Thy service! May I now trust and rely upon the arm of Omnipotence, the mercies of the Lord! Give me strength, Lord, to this end. Amen.

Your Great God Cares for You

15

I BELIEVE that we fail to bring little troubles to God, and perhaps on account of their being so little, we fancy that we must not mention them to the Most High. This is but the fruit of our pride, for how do we know that our great things are so great as we think them to be? and are not our little things, after all, but the fractions of a considerable sum to such little creatures as ourselves? These little, little things are of momentous concern to such little ones as we are; and the God that stoops to us at all has already brought himself down in condescension so low that we need not fear that we shall bring him lower. No, you may go to him if you like about that lost key, or about that child's swelling finger, or about that word that irritated you just now. There is nothing little to a father in the thing that troubles his little child; and your great God, having once condescended to observe and care for you, numbering the very hairs of your head, and not suffering a sparrow to fall to the ground without his purpose and decree, will not think that you intrude upon him if you bring your daily troubles to him.

Prayer

OUR Father, Thy children who know Thee delight themselves in Thy presence. We are never happier than when we are near Thee. We have found a little heaven in prayer. It has eased our load to tell Thee of its weight; it has relieved our wound to tell Thee of its smart; it has restored our spirit to confess to Thee its wanderings. For thy great and loving care, we thank Thee. Amen.

Prayer As Resource and Strength

16 The Lord of hosts is with us; the God of
Jacob is our refuge. Selah. — *Psalm 46:7*

A PEOPLE who can pray can never be
overcome, because their reserve forces can
never be exhausted. Go into battle, my
brother; and if you be vanquished with the
strength you have, prayer shall call up
another legion, yea, twenty legions of
angels, and the foe shall marvel to see un-
defeated adversaries still holding the field.
If ten thousand saints were burned tomorrow, their dying prayers would make
the church rise like a phoenix from her
ashes. Who, therefore, can stand against
a people whose prayers enlist God in their
quarrel? "The Lord of Hosts is with us;
the God of Jacob is our refuge." We cry
unto the Lord, and he heareth us; he
breaketh through the ranks of the foe; he
giveth us triumph in the day of battle:
therefore, terrible as an army with ban-
ners are those who wield the weapon of
prayer.

Prayer

W E thank Thee, Lord, that we have not only found benefit in prayer, but in the answers to it we have been greatly enriched. Thou hast opened Thy hid treasures to the voice of prayer; Thou hast supplied our necessities as soon as ever we have cried unto Thee; yea, we have found it true: "Before they call I will answer, and while they are yet speaking I will hear." Amen.

The Providence of God

17

Be strong and of good courage, fear not, nor be afraid of them; for the Lord thy God, he it is that doth go with thee; he will not fail thee, nor forsake thee. — Deuteronomy 31:6

W E believe in the providence of God, but we do not believe half enough in it. Remember that Omnipotence has servants everywhere, set in their places at every point of the road. In the old days of the post horses there were always swift horses ready to carry onward the king's mail.

It is wonderful how God has His relays of providential agents; how when He has done with one there is always another ready to take his place. Sometimes you have found one friend fail you — he is just dead and buried. "Ah!" you say, "what shall I do?" Well, well, **God knows how to carry on the purposes of His providence;** He will raise up another. How strikingly punctual providence is! You and I make appointments and miss them by half an hour; but **God never missed an appointment yet!** God never is before His time though **we** often wish He were; but He is never behind — no, **not by one tick of the clock.**

And now, trembler, wherefore are you afraid? "Fear thou not; for I am with thee." **All the mysterious arrangements of providence work for our good.**

40

Prayer

O LORD, we would delight ourselves in Thee this day. Give us faith and love and hope that with these three graces we may draw very near to the Triune God. Thou wilt keep us, Thou wilt preserve us, Thou wilt feed us, Thou wilt lead us, and Thou wilt bring us to the mind of God, and there wilt Thou show us Thy love, and in the glory everlasting and boundless, there wilt Thou make us know and taste and feel the joys that cannot be expressed. Amen.

Never Get Disengaged from Your Guide

18 *But as for me, my feet were almost gone; my steps had well-nigh slipped.—Psalm 73:2*

WE were at the foot of Mount Blanc in the village of Chammouni. A sad thing had happened the day before. A young physician had determined to reach the heights of Mount Blanc. He accomplished the feat and the little village was illuminated in his honor; on the mountainside a flag was floating that told of his victory.

After he had ascended, and descended as far as the hut, he wanted to be released from his guide; he wanted to be free from the rope, and insisted on going on alone. The guide was compelled to yield. The young man had gone only a short distance when his foot slipped on the ice and he could not stop himself from sliding down the icy steeps. The rope was gone, so the guide could not hold him nor pull him back.

The bells had been rung, the village had been illuminated in honor of his success; but alas, in a fatal moment he refused to be guided; he was tired of the rope.

Do you get tired of the rope? God's providences hold us, restrain us, and we get tired sometimes. We need a guide, and shall until the dangerous paths are over. **Never get disengaged from your Guide.**

Prayer

O THOU whom my soul loveth, daily meet me; sanctify me, prepare me, help me to bring forth fruit and to be Thine forever! Hold Thou me by Thy free Spirit, and pour down upon me more love to Thee. Thou art the sole desire of my heart. May it always be so and do Thou keep me ... then I need fear no fall. Amen.

One Can Be Too Ambitious

19

Trust in the Lord with all thine heart; and lean not unto thine own understanding. In all thy ways acknowledge him, and he shall direct thy paths. — *Proverbs 3:5-6*

AMBITION is like the sea which swallows all the rivers and is none the fuller; or like the grave which craves for bodies. It is not like an amphora, which being full receives no more; but its fullness swells it till a still greater vacuum is formed.

In all probability, Napoleon never longed for a sceptre till he had gained the baton, nor dreamed of being emperor of Europe till he had gained the crown of France. Caligula, with the world at his feet, was mad with a longing for the moon, and could he have gained it the imperial lunatic would have coveted the sun. It is in vain to feed a fire which grows the more voracious the more it is supplied with fuel; he who lives to satisfy his ambition has before him the labor of Sisyphus, who rolled up hill an ever-rebounding stone.

Could we know the secret heartbreaks and weariness of ambitious men, we should need no Wolsey's voice crying, "I charge thee, fling away ambition," but we should flee from it as from the most accursed blood-thirsty vampire which ever uprose from the caverns of hell.

Prayer

OUR God, we are Thine. Thou art ours.
We are now concerned in one business;
we are leagued together for one battle.
Thy battle is our battle, and our fight is
Thine. Help us, we pray Thee. Thou who
didst strengthen Michael and his angels to
cast out the dragon and his angels, help
poor flesh and blood that we also may
conquer every foe. Amen.

On Reading the Bible with Delight

20 And I will delight myself in thy commandments, which I have loved. — *Psalm 119:47*

WHEN Mr. Hone, who wrote the "Everyday Book," and was of skeptical views, was travelling through Wales, he stopped at a cottage to ask for a drink of water, and a little girl answered him, "Oh, yes! sir, I have no doubt mother will give you some milk if you like. Come in." He went in and sat down. The little girl was reading her Bible. Mr. Hone said, "Well, my little girl, do you find reading that a task?" "No, sir," she replied, "it is no task to read the Bible; I love the Bible." "And why do you love the Bible?" said he. Her simple, childlike answer was, "I thought everybody loved the Bible." Her own love of the precious volume had made her innocently believe that everybody else was equally delighted to read God's Word. Mr. Hone was so touched with the sincerity of that expression, that he read the Bible himself, and instead of being an opponent to the things of God, came to be a friend of divine truth.

Prayer

LORD, we are not what we want to be. This is our sorrow. Oh! that Thou wouldest, by Thy Spirit, help us in the walks of life to adorn the doctrine of God our Savior in all things. As men of business, as work-people, as parents, as children, as servants, as masters, whatever we may be, may we be such that Christ may look upon us with pleasure. May His joy be in us, for then only can our joy be full. Amen.

Christ's Welcome

21

Come unto me, all ye that labour and are heavy laden, and I will give you rest. — Matthew 11:28

WE are told that in stormy weather it is not unusual for small birds to be blown out of sight of land on to the sea. They are often seen by voyagers far from the coast, hovering over the masts on weary wings as if they wanted to alight and rest themselves, but fearing to do so. A traveller tells us that on one occasion, a little lark, which followed the ship for a considerable distance, was at last compelled through sheer weariness to alight. He was so worn out as to be easily caught. The warmth of the hand was so agreeable to him that he sat down on it, burying his little cold feet in his feathers, and looking about with his bright eye not in the least afraid, and as if feeling assured that he had been cast amongst good kind people whom he had no occasion to be so backward in trusting. This is a touching picture of the soul who is aroused by the Spirit of God and blown out of its own reckoning by the winds of conviction; and the warm reception which the weary little bird received at the hands of the passengers conveys but a faint idea of that welcome which will greet the worn out, sin sick souls who will commit themselves into the hands of the only Savior.

Prayer

LORD, here am I. Thou hast said that Christ is able to save to the uttermost them that come unto God by him. I am a soul that wants saving to the uttermost, and here I am; I have come, Lord, save me. Amen.

Neutrality Impossible for the Christian

22 For none of us liveth to himself, and no man dieth to himself. — *Romans 14:7*

IT appears that Themistocles, when a boy, was full of spirit and fire, quick of apprehension, naturally inclined to bold attempts, and likely to make a great statesman. His hours of leisure and vacation he spent not, like other boys, in idleness and play, but he was always inventing and composing declamations, the subjects of which were either impeachments or defenses of some of his schoolfellows; so that his master would often say, "Boy, you will be nothing common or indifferent; you will either be a blessing or a curse to the community."

So remember, you who profess to be followers of the Lord Jesus, that to you indifference is impossible; you **must** bless the church and the world by your holiness, or you will curse them both by your hypocrisy and inconsistency.

In the visible church it is most true that "no man liveth unto himself, and no man dieth unto himself."

Prayer

LORD, look on me this day, and nerve
me for its duties and conflicts. Let me by
faith exercise the power with which Thou
hast entrusted me. At thy command I go
to do thy will; I am assured that Thou
wilt conquer by me. Amen.

If We Carry with Us Our Own Hell

23 They have deeply corrupted themselves, as in the days of Gibeah: therefore he will remember their iniquity, he will visit their sins. — *Hosea 9:9*

GEORGE Shadford wrote: "One day a friend took me to see a hermit in the woods. After some difficulty we found his hermitage, which was a little place like a hog-sty, built of several pieces of wood, covered with bark of trees, and his bed consisted of dry leaves. There was a narrow beaten path about twenty or thirty yards in length by the side of it, where he frequently walked to meditate."

"If one offered him food, he would take it; but if money was offered him, he would be angry. If anything was spoken which he did not like, he broke out into violent passion. He had lived in this cell seven cold winters, and after all his ... separating from the rest of mankind, still corrupt nature was all alive within him."

Alas! what will it avail us whether we are in England or America, whether we live amongst mankind, or retire into a hermitage, if we still carry with us our own hell, our corrupt evil tempers? Without a new heart and a right spirit, no condition can deliver a man from his sins. Neither publicity nor solitude avails anything until grace prevails with us. The devil can tempt in the wilderness as well as in the crowd. We want not hermitages but heavenly-mindedness.

Prayer

LORD, though I halt in faith, in prayer, in praise, in service, and in patience, save me, I beseech Thee. Only Thou canst save such a cripple as I am. Lord, let me not perish because I am among the slow, but gather up by Thy grace the slowest of Thy pilgrims — even me. Amen.

Covetousness

24

Thou shalt not covet thy neighbour's house, thou shalt not covet thy neighbour's wife, nor his manservant, nor his maidservant, nor his ox, nor his ass, nor any thing that is thy neighbour's. — *Exodus 20:17*

BEWARE of growing covetousness, for of all sins this is one of the most insidious. It is like the silting up of a river. As the stream comes down from the land, it brings with it sand and earth, and deposits all these at its mouth, so that by degrees, unless the conservators watch it carefully, it will block itself up, and leave no channel for ships of great burden. By daily deposit it imperceptibly creates a bar which is dangerous to navigation.

Many a man when he begins to accumulate wealth commences at the same moment to ruin his soul, and the more he acquires, the more closely he blocks up his liberality, which is, so to speak, the very mouth of spiritual life. Instead of doing more for God he does less; the more he saves the more he wants, and the more he wants of this world the less he cares for the world to come.

Prayer

WHAT have we to do with idols any more, O God? Thou hast seen and observed us. Thou knowest where the difficulty lies. Help us against it, and may we now come boldly into the Holy place.... Peradventure some of us are attracted to the world; come near to kill the influence of this world with Thy superior power. Amen.

The Evils of Inactivity

25

But ye, brethren, be not weary in well-doing. — *II Thessalonians 3:13*

WHAT a mournful sight the observer may see in some of the outskirts of a huge city: row after row of houses all untenanted and forlorn. The owners had far better rent them at the lowest price than suffer them to remain empty, for the boys make targets of the windows, enterprising purveyors for the marine store shops rend off all the lead, thieves purloin every movable fitting, damp swells the window frames and doors, and mustiness makes the whole place wretched to all the senses; the district gets a bad name which it probably never loses. Better a poor tenant than a house running to ruin unused.

The similitude may well suggest the desirableness of an object and a service to those Christians whose time is wasted in slothful ease. All sorts of mischief happen to unoccupied professors of religion; there is no evil from which they are secure; better would it be for them to accept the lowest occupation for the Lord Jesus, than remain the victim of inaction.

Prayer

OUR Father, which art in heaven; we would offer prayer for those who never think of Thee; who, though created by Thee, are strangers to Thee; who are fed by Thy bounty, and yet never lift their voices to Thee but live for self, for the world, for Satan, for sin. Father, these cannot pray for themselves for they are dead; Thy quickened children pray for them. These will not come to Thee, for, like sheep, they are lost; but do Thou seek them Father, and bring them back. Amen.

Generosity

26 Look not every man on his own things, but every man also on the things of others. — Philippians 2:4

ONE incident gives high proof of the native generosity of the painter Turner. He was one of the hanging committee, as the phrase goes, of the Royal Academy. The walls were full when Turner's attention was attracted by a picture sent in by an unknown provincial artist by the name of Bird. 'A good picture,' he exclaimed. 'It must be hung up and exhibited.' 'Impossible!' responded the committee of academicians. 'The arrangement cannot be disturbed. Quite impossible!' 'A good picture,' iterated Turner, 'it must be hung up'; and finding his colleagues to be as obstinate as himself, he took down one of his own pictures, and hung up Bird's in its place."

Would to God that in far more instances the like spirit ruled among servants of the Lord Jesus. The desire to honor others and to give others a fair opportunity to rise should lead ministers of distinction to give place to less eminent men to whom it may be of essential service to become better known. We are not to look every man on his own things, but every man also on the things of others.

Prayer

GIVE us Thy Spirit, O Savior, more
fully, that we may live Thy life while we
are here among the sons of men, for as
Thou art, even so also are we in this
world, and we wish the parallel to become
more close and perfect every day! Amen.

Chronic Discontent

27 And one said, Be content, I pray thee. . . .
— II Kings 6:3

SOME people are never content with their lot, no matter what happens. Clouds and darkness are over their heads, alike whether it rain or shine. To them every incident is an accident, and every accident a calamity. Even when they have their own way, they like it no better than your way, and indeed consider their most voluntary acts as matters of compulsion. We saw a striking illustration the other day of the infirmity we speak of in the conduct of a child, about three years old. He was crying because his mother had shut the parlor door. "Poor thing," said a neighbor compassionately, "you have shut the child **out**." "It's all the same to him," said the mother; "he would cry if I called him **in** and then shut the door. It is a peculiarity of that boy, that if he is left rather suddenly on either side of a door, he considers himself shut out, and rebels accordingly." There are older children who take the same view of things.

Prayer

O LORD God, help me now really to worship Thee. Help me to forget my cares. Enable me to escape the world for a moment so that I may get rid of all its down-dragging tendencies. Fix my eyes upon Jesus so that I may rejoice as if He were here before my very eyes. Through Christ my Lord. Amen.

God's Lovingkindness

28

How excellent is thy lovingkindness, O God!
— Psalm 36:7

I REMEMBER well being taken one day to see a gorgeous palace at Venice, where every piece of furniture was made with most exquisite taste, and of the richest material, where statues and pictures of enormous price abounded on all hands, and the floor of each room was paved with mosaics of marvellous art of extraordinary value. As I was shown from room to room and allowed to roam amid the treasures by its courteous owner, I felt a considerable timidity; I was afraid to sit anywhere, nor did I hardly dare to put down my foot, or rest my hand to lean. Everything seemed to be too good for ordinary mortals like myself; but when one is introduced into the gorgeous palace of infinite goodness, costlier and fairer far, one gazes wonderingly with reverential awe at the matchless vision. "How excellent is thy lovingkindness, O God!" "I am not worthy of the least of all thy benefits. Oh! the depths of the love and goodness of the Lord."

Prayer

WE desire to praise the name of the Lord with our whole heart, for we have tasted that the Lord is gracious. Truly Thou hast delivered us from the gulf of dark despair, wherein we wretched sinners lay. Thou hast brought us up also out of the horrible pit and out of the miry clay; Thou hast set our feet upon a rock and the new song which Thou hast put into our mouths we would not stifle, but we would bless the Lord whose mercy endureth forever. Amen.

Diligence

29 And beside this, giving all diligence, add to your faith virtue; and to virtue knowledge. — II Peter 1:5

SELECT a large box and place in it as many cannon balls as it will hold; it is after a fashion full but it will hold more. ... Bring a quantity of marbles; very many of these may be packed in the spaces between the larger globes. The box is full but full only in a sense, for it can contain more. There are interstices in abundance into which you may shake a considerable quantity of small shot. Now, you say, the chest is filled beyond all question; but wait — there is still more. While you cannot put in another shot or marble, much less another cannon ball, you will find several pounds of sand will slide down between the larger materials. ...

When there is no space for the great, there may be room for the little; where the little cannot enter, the less can make its way; and where the less is shut out, the least of all may find ample room.

Now the diligent church worker may not be able to give more talks or teach more lessons. Still there must be stray moments which might hold a vast amount of little usefulness. What a wealth of minor good, as we may think it to be, might be shaken down into the interstices of ten years work, which might prove to be as precious in result as the greater works of the same period.

Prayer

O, THOU precious Lord Jesus Christ, we do adore Thee with all our hearts. Thou art Lord of all. We bless Thee for becoming man that Thou mightest be our next of kin, and being next of kin we bless Thee for taking us into marriage union with Thyself and for redeeming us and our inheritance from the captivity into which we were sold. Thou hast paid Thy life for Thy people; Thou hast ransomed Thy folk with Thy heart's blood. Be Thou, therefore, forever beloved and adored. Amen.

To Conquer the World for the Christ

30   The fruit of the righteous is a tree of life; and he that winneth souls is wise. — *Proverbs 11:30*

I ONCE heard a story of an American who declared he could fight the whole British army. When he was asked how he could draw so long a bow as that, he said, "Why, this is what I would do: I know I am the best swordsman in the world, so I would go and challenge one Britisher, and kill him; then take another, and kill him. Thus," said he, "I only want time enough and I would kill the whole British army." It was a ridiculous boast, but there is something in it which I could not bring out so well in any other way. If we want to conquer the world for the Lord Jesus Christ, rest assured we must do it in the Yankee's fashion; we must take men one by one, and these must be brought to Christ, or otherwise the great mass must remain untouched. Do not imagine for a moment that you are going to convert a nation at once; you are to convert the men of that nation, one by one, through the power of God's Holy Spirit. It is not for you to suit your machinery and arrange your plans for the moving of a mass as such; you must look to the salvation of the units.

Prayer

LORD, Lord, if there be a heart that is saying, "Now, behold I yield; lo! at Thy feet rebellion's weapons I lay down, and cease to be Thy foe, Thou King of kings" — if there be one saying this — bring that willing sinner in now! May there be no longer delay, but may this be the time when, once for all, the great transaction shall be done and he shall be the Lord's. Amen.

Resignation, the Root of Peace

31

Commit thy works unto the Lord, and thy thoughts shall be established. — *Proverbs* 16:3

THE habit of resignation is the root of peace.

A godly child had a ring given him by his mother, and he greatly prized it, but on one occasion he unhappily lost his ring and he cried bitterly. But recapturing his composure, he stepped aside and prayed; after which his sister laughingly said to him, "Brother, what is the good of praying about a ring — will praying bring back your ring?" "Perhaps not," said he, "but praying has done this for me; it has made me quite willing to do without the ring if it is God's will; and is not that almost as good as having it?"

Thus faith quiets us by resignation, as a babe is hushed in his mother's bosom. Faith makes us quite willing to do without the mercy which once we prized; and when the heart is content to be without the outward blessing, it is as happy as it would be with it; for it is at rest.

Prayer

WE come to Thee this day with a supreme joy; we speak of Thee as our "exceeding joy" and our own God. Give us a sense of property in Thyself. May we come near to Thee, having no doubt and nothing whatsoever that shall spoil the beautiful simplicity of a childlike faith which looks up into the great face of God and saith, "Our Father, which art in heaven." Amen.

Haben Sie Keine Schules?

32

To know wisdom and instruction; to perceive the words of understanding; to receive the instruction of wisdom, justice, and judgment, and equity; to give subtilty to the simple, to the young man knowledge and discretion.
— *Proverbs 1:2-4*

By order of government the roads in Prussia are lined on each side with fruit trees. Riding once, early in September, from Berlin to Halle, an American traveller noticed that some of the trees had a wisp of straw attached to them. He inquired of the coachman what it meant. He replied that those trees bore choice fruits, and the straw was a notice to the public not to take fruit from those trees without special permission. "I fear," said the traveller, "that in my country such a notice would be but an invitation to roguish boys to attack those very trees." **"Haben Sie keine Schules?"** ("Have you no schools?") was his significant rejoinder.

Rest assured, dear reader, that next to godliness, education is the mainstay of order. Let us thank God daily for schools; and let us pray for more Christian teachers and plead at the throne of grace for righteous institutions of learning.

Prayer

BLESSED art Thou, O God; teach us Thy statutes! Because Thou art the infinitely blessed One, Thou canst impart blessing, and Thou art infinitely willing to do so, and therefore do we approach Thee with great confidence, through Jesus Christ Thy Son, whom Thou hast made blessed for evermore. Amen.

Judge Not

33

Judge not, that ye be not judged. For with what judgment ye judge, ye shall be judged: and with what measure ye mete, it shall be measured to you again. — *Matthew 7:1-2*

W HO respects the wretch who has no respect for others? whose only life is to pull other men's characters to pieces? I have seen such men and women who seem to have a propensity to observe that which is evil in another more than that which is good. Let me ask this question: My friend, it is all very well for you to have those eyes so sharp, and to wear those magnifying glasses for other people, but "are there not with you, even with you, sins against the Lord your God?" What about your own life? I will tell you something about it. Whatever you think of other people is true of yourself; that is an invariable rule. We always measure other people's corn with our own bushel, and if you think you find other people's corn gritty, the dirt was originally your own. Depend upon it, that your judgment of others will be God's judgment of you, for with what measure ye mete the same shall be measured to you again.

Prayer

O GOD, push us towards purity, for we crave after it; help us to live close to Thy Spirit, for we would be utterly delivered from the things of the flesh, that we may in spirit, soul, and body, be a cleansed temple fit for the indwelling of the Holy One of Israel. Lord help us, we pray Thee, in our daily life, to be as Christ was. May we seek in all ways the good of our fellow men and the glory of our God. Amen.

34   . . . Beware ye of the leaven of the Pharisees, which is hypocrisy. — *Luke 12:1*

THIS age is full of shams. If you walked through the streets of London, you might imagine that all the shops were built of marble, and that all the doors were made of mahogany and woods of the rarest kinds; and yet you soon discover that there is scarce a piece of any of these precious fabrics to be found anywhere, but that everything is grained, painted and varnished. I find no fault with this, except that it is an outward type of an inward evil that exists.

As it is in our streets, so it is everywhere: graining, painting, and gilding are at an enormous premium. Counterfeit has at length attained to such an eminence that it is with the utmost difficulty that you can detect it. Specially is this the case in religious matters. There was once an age of intolerant bigotry, when every man was weighed in the balance, and if he was not precisely up to the orthodox standard of the day, the fire devoured him; but in this age of charity, and of most proper charity, we are very apt to allow the counterfeit to pass, and to imagine that outward show is really as beneficial as inward reality. If ever there was a time when it was needful to say, "Beware ye of the leaven of the Pharisees, which is hypocrisy," it is now.

Prayer

LORD, preserve me from everything that would dishonor the name of the Christ that I bear. Lord make me holy. Make me holy; cleanse the inside and let the outside be clean too. Amen.

Ivy in Hampton Court

35

Then beware lest thou forget the Lord which brought thee forth out of the land of Egypt, from the house of bondage. — *Deuteronomy 6:12*

IN the gardens of Hampton Court you will see many trees entirely vanquished and nigh strangled by huge coils of ivy. There is no untwisting the folds, they are too giant-like and fast fixed, and every hour the rootlets of the climber are sucking the life out of the unhappy tree. Yet there was a day when the ivy was a tiny aspirant, only asking a little aid in climbing; had it been denied then, the tree had never become its victim; but by degrees the humble weakling grew in strength and arrogance, and at last it assumed the mastery, and the tall tree became the prey of the creeping, insinuating destroyer.

The moral is obvious. Sorrowfully do we remember many noble characters which have been ruined little by little, by insinuating habits. Drink has been the ivy in many cases. Reader, see to it, lest some slowly advancing sin overpower you: men who are murdered by slow poisoning die just as surely as those who take arsenic.

Prayer

OUR Father, we are very weak. Worst of all we are very wicked if left to ourselves, and we soon fall prey to the enemy. Therefore help us. Amen.

Quiet and Companionable Lions

36 When a man's ways please the Lord, He maketh even his enemies to be at peace with him. — *Proverbs 16:7*

I MUST see that my ways please the Lord. Even then I shall have enemies; and, perhaps, all the more certainly because I endeavored to do that which is right. But what a promise Proverbs 16:7 is! The Lord will make the wrath of men to praise him, and abate it so that it shall not distress me. He can constrain an enemy to desist from harming me, even though he has a mind to do so. This He did with Laban, who pursued Jacob, but did not dare touch him; or he can subdue the wrath of the enemy, and make him friendly, as He did with Esau who met Jacob in a brotherly manner, though Jacob had dreaded that he would smite him and his family with the sword. The Lord can also convert a furious adversary into a brother in Christ, and a fellow worker, as he did Saul of Tarsus.

Happy is the man whose enemies are made to be to him what the lions were to Daniel in the den, quiet and companionable! When I meet death, which is called the last enemy, I pray that I may be at peace. Only let my great care be to please the Lord in all things. Oh, for faith and holiness; for these are a pleasure unto the Most High!

Prayer

LORD, purify us in head, heart and hand; and if it be needful that we should be put into the fire to be refined as silver is refined, we would even welcome the fire if we may be rid of the dross. Lord save us from sins of temperament and from the sins of our surroundings. Save us from ourselves and grant us especially to have the light of love strong within us. Amen.

On Going to Bed with Your Boots On

37

Let us walk honestly, as in the day; not in rioting and drunkeness, not in chambering and wantonness, not in strife and envying. But put ye on the Lord Jesus Christ, and make not provision for the flesh, to fulfill the lusts thereof. — *Romans 13:13-14*

A TRAVELLER in Venezuela illustrates the readiness of men to lay their faults on the locality, or on anything rather than themselves, by the story of a hard drinker who came home one night in such a condition that he could not for some time find his hammock. When this feat was accomplished, he tried in vain to get off his big riding boots. After many fruitless efforts he lay down in his hammock and soliloquized aloud, "Well, I have travelled all the world over; I lived five years in Cuba, four in Jamaica, five in Brazil; I have travelled through Spain and Portugal, and been in Africa, but I never yet was in such an abominable country as this, where a man must go to bed with his boots on."

Commonly enough are we told by evil-doers in excuse for their sins that no man could do otherwise were he in their position; that there is no living at their trade honestly, that in such a street shops must be open on a Sunday, that their health required an excursion to Brighton on the Sabbath because their labors were so severe, that nobody could be religious in the house in which they were engaged, and so on, all about as truthful as the soliloquy of the drunkard of Venezuela.

Prayer

Now, Lord, we confess our guilt before Thee with tenderness of heart, and we pray Thee seal home to this believer that full and free, that perfect and irreversible charter of forgiveness which Thou givest to all who put their trust in Jesus Christ. Lord! Thou hast said, "If we confess our sins, Thou art merciful and just to forgive us our sins and to save us from all unrighteousness." We thank Thee. Amen.

Idle Christians and Temptation

38

Behold, this was the iniquity of thy sister Sodom, pride, fulness of bread, and abundance of idleness was in her and in her daughters, neither did she strenghten the hand of the poor and needy. — Ezekiel 16:49

NOTICE the invention of some country people to catch wasps. They will put a little sweet liquor into a long and narrow-necked vial. The do-nothing wasp comes by, smells the sweet liquor, plunges in and is drowned. But the bee comes by, and if she does stop for a moment to smell, yet she enters not, because she has honey of her own to make; she is too busy in the work of the commonwealth to indulge herself with the tempting sweets.

Master Greenham, a Puritan minister of the gospel, was once waited upon by a woman who was greatly tempted. Upon making inquiries into her way of life, he found she had little to do and Greenham said, "That is the secret of your being so much tempted. Sister, if you are very busy, Satan may tempt you, but he will not easily prevail, and he will soon give up the attempt."

Idle Christians are not tempted of the devil so much as they tempt the devil to tempt them.

Prayer

O LORD, may every breath of mine be for Thee. May every minute be spent in Thy service. Help me to live while I live, and while I am busy in the world as I must be, for I am called to it, grant me a share in making it a better place in which to live. Through Jesus Christ, my Lord. Amen.

The Benefit of Sorrow

39 Verily, verily, I say unto you, Except a corn of wheat fall into the ground and die, it abideth alone; but if it die, it bringeth forth much fruit. — John 12:24

Two seeds lie before us — the one is warmed in the sun, the other falls from the sower's hand into the cold dark earth, and there it lies buried beneath the soil. That seed which suns itself in the noontide beam may rejoice in the light in which it basks, but it is liable to be devoured by the bird; and certainly nothing can come of it, however long it may linger above ground. But the other seed, hidden beneath the clods in a damp, dark sepulchre, soon swells, germinates, bursts its sheath, upheaves the mould, springs up a green blade, buds, blossoms becomes a flower, exhales perfume, and loads the wings of every wind. Better far for the seed to pass into the earth and die, than to lie in the sunshine and produce no fruit.

So it is with you. The future, in its sorrow, shall be as a sowing in a fertile land. Tears shall moisten, grace shall increase, and you shall grow up in the likeness of your Lord unto perfection of holiness, to be such a flower of God's own planting as even angels shall delight to gaze upon in the day of your transplanting to celestial soil.

Prayer

OH! keep us, Lord. This life is full of
trial. Sometimes we are perplexed.... Let
not the enemy lead us to do or think
amiss. Sometimes we are blessed with
prosperity. Lord, let it not be a curse to
us. Let us know how to abound as well as
how to suffer loss. In all things instruct us
to glorify God, not only with all that we
are but all that we have.

On Speculating upon the Prophecies

40

Every prudent man dealeth with knowledge: but a fool layeth open his folly. — *Proverbs 13:16*

WHILE a minister of my acquaintance was riding in a railway carriage, he was saluted by a member of an exceedingly speculative sect. "Pray, sir," said a member of the sect, "what is your opinion of the seven trumpets?" "I am not sure," said the preacher, "that I understand your question, but I hope you will comprehend mine: What think you of the fact that your seven children are growing up without God and without hope? You have a Bible-reading in your house for your neighbors, but no family prayer for your children."

The nail was fastened in a sure place; enough candor of mind remained in the professor to enable him to profit by the timely rebuke.

It is greatly to be desired that Christians who are so much given to speculate upon the prophecies, would turn their thoughts and leisure to the perishing myriads by whom we are surrounded, and sow in the fields of evangelization rather than in the cloudland of guess-work interpretation.

Prayer

OUR prayer today, O God, is for the many efforts for Kingdom building. May they be good wherever they are. We pray for all churches; Lord, revive them all. Wherever Christ is preached, may it be proved that He draws all men unto Him. May the preaching of Christ in these days be peculiarly efficacious. Oh! that Thou wouldst raise up many who would preach Christ simply and boldly. Amen.

The True Ground of Faith

41 For he remembered his holy promise, and Abraham his servant. — *Psalm 105:42*

GOD is to be trusted for what He is, and not for what He is not. We may confidently expect Him to act according to His nature, but never contrary to it. To dream that God will do this and that because we wish that He would is not faith, but fanaticism. Faith can only stand upon truth. We may be sure that God will so act as to honor His own justice, mercy, wisdom, power — in a word, so as to be Himself. Beyond all doubt He will fulfill His promises; and when faith grasps a promise she is on sure ground.

To believe that God will give us what He has never promised to give is mere dreaming. Faith without a promise revealed or implied is folly. Yea, though our trust should cry itself hoarse in prayer, it should be nonetheless a vain dotard if it had no word of God to warrant it. Happily, the promises and unveilings of Scripture are ample for every real emergency; but when unrestrained credence catches at every whim of its own crazy imagination and thinks to see it realized, the disappointment is not to be wondered at.

It is ours to believe the sure things of God's revelation, but we are not to waste a grain of precious reliance upon anything outside of that circle.

Prayer

O SAVIOR, reveal Thyself anew. Teach us a little more, help us to go a little deeper into the divine mystery. May we grip Thee and grasp Thee; may we be in Thee as a branch is in the stem; may we bear fruit from Thee. Without Thee we can do nothing. Amen.

We Must Pray to Pray

42 Therefore turn thou to thy God: keep mercy and judgment, and wait on thy God continually. — *Hosea 12:6*

No doubt by praying we learn to pray. The more we pray the oftener we can pray, and the better we can pray.

Great power in prayer is within our reach, but we must go to work to obtain it. Let us never imagine that Abraham could have interceded so successfully for Sodom if he had not been all his lifetime in the practice of communion with God.

Jacob's all-night at Peniel was not the first occasion upon which he had met his God. We may even look upon our Lord's most wonderful prayer with His disciples before His Passion as the flower and fruit of His many periods of devotion.

The prayer of Elias which shut up heaven and afterwards opened its floodgates, was one of a long series of mighty prevailings with God. Oh, that Christian men would remember this! Perseverance in prayer is necessary to prevalence in prayer.

Those great intercessors, who are not so often mentioned as they ought to be in connection with confessors and martyrs, were nevertheless the grandest benefactors of the church; but it was only by abiding at the mercy seat that they attained to be such channels of mercy. We must pray to pray, and continue in prayer that our prayers may continue.

Prayer

OUR Father, Thou dost hear us when we pray. Thou hast provided an advocate and intercessor in heaven now; we cannot come to Thee unless Thy Holy Spirit shall suggest desire. Help us while we plead. Amen.

God's Grace Is Sufficient

43
And he said unto me, My grace is sufficient
for thee. . . . — II Corinthians 12:9

THE other evening I was riding home
after a heavy day's work. I felt very
wearied, and sore depressed, when swiftly,
and suddenly as a lightning flash, that
text came to me, "My grace is sufficient
for thee." I reached home and looked it
up in the original, and at last it came to
me in this way, "MY grace is sufficient
for thee"; and I said, "I should think it
is, Lord," and burst out laughing. I never
fully understood what the holy laughter
of Abraham was until then. It seemed to
make unbelief so absurd. It was as though
some little fish, being very thirsty, was
troubled about drinking the river dry, and
Father Thomas said, "Drink away, little
fish, my stream is sufficient for thee." Or,
it seemed after the seven years of plenty,
a mouse feared it might die of famine; and
Joseph might say, "Cheer up, little mouse,
my granaries are sufficient for thee."
Again, I imagined a man away up yonder,
in a lofty mountain, saying to himself, "I
breathe so many cubic feet of air every
year, I fear I shall exhaust the oxygen in
the atmosphere," but the earth might say,
"Breathe away, O man, and fill the lungs
ever, my atmosphere is sufficient for thee."

Oh, brethren, be great believers! Little
faith will bring your souls to Heaven, but
great faith will bring Heaven to your souls.

Prayer

W E do accept Thee, Lord Jesus, to be
made unto us wisdom, righteousness, sanc-
tification, and redemption. We will not
look outside of Thee for anything, for
everything is in Thee. Amen.

God Is Near

44

Thou art near, O Lord; and all thy commandments are truth. — Psalm 119:151

TWO friends agree never to go farther apart than they can communicate with one another by telegraph. One of them has crossed the Atlantic, and resides in the United States, or in the far west, but still he has only to go to the office, where a wire can be sent and a message will flash to his friend in England, and tell him his needs.

This is just the compact God has made with his people: they shall never go where there is not a telegraphic communication between them and himself. You may be out at sea, or in Australia, but the communication of prayer is always open between your soul and God, and if you were commanded to ride on the wings of the morning to the uttermost parts of the sea, or if for a while you had to make your bed in the abyss, if you were his child, still would you be able to reach his heart.

Prayer

OUR longing, O God, is to feel Thy presence, and it is the heaven of heavens that Thou art near. The sick bed is soft when Thou art near, and the house of prayer when Thou art present is none other than the house of God, and it is the very gate of heaven. Amen.

Good Solid Doctrine

45 For I give you good doctrine, forsake ye not my law. — *Proverbs 4:2*

IT is a great thing to begin the Christian life by believing good solid doctrine. Some people have received twenty different "gospels" in as many years; how many more they will accept before they get to their journey's end, it would be difficult to predict. I thank God that He early taught me the gospel; and I have been so perfectly satisfied with it, that I do not want to know any other. Constant change of creed is sure loss. If a tree has to be taken up two or three times a year, you will not need to build a very large loft in which to store the apples. When people are always shifting their doctrinal principles, they are not likely to bring forth much fruit to the glory of God. It is good for young believers to begin with a firm hold upon those great fundamental doctrines which the Lord has taught in His Word.

Prayer

OUR Father, save this age from its own intellectual pride. Give back the spirit of simple faith in Christ, for we desire His glory. "For thine is the kingdom, and the power, and the glory, forever and ever. Amen."

Soldiers of Jesus Christ

46

No man that warreth entangleth himself with
the affairs of this life; that he man please
him who hath chosen him to be a soldier.
— II Timothy 2:4

WELLINGTON sent word to his troops
one night, "Ciudad Rodrigo must be taken
tonight." And what do you think was the
commentary of the British soldiers appointed for the attack? "Then," said they
all, "we will do it." So when our great
Captain sends round, as he does, the word
of command, "Go ye into all the world and
preach the gospel to every creature," if
we were all good soldiers of the cross, we
should say at once, "We will do it."

However hard the task, since God himself is with us to be our Captain, and
Jesus the Priest of the Most High is with
us to sound the trumpet, we will do it in
Jehovah's name. May such dauntless resolution fire your imaginations and may you
thus prove yourselves "good soldiers of
Jesus Christ."

Prayer

STRENGTHEN in Thy servants, O God, all that is good and right. Sanctify us to Thy service and hold us to it. Make us like Thyself; bring us near Thyself and in all things glorify Thyself in us, whether we live or die. Amen. ·

The Holy Spirit, Guide to Truth

47   He will guide you into all truth. — *John* 16:13

TRUTH may be compared to some cave or grotto, with wondrous stalactites hanging from the roof and others abounding in marvels. Before entering the cavern you inquire for a guide, who comes with his lighted torch. He conducts you down to a considerable depth, and you find yourself in the midst of the cave. He leads you through different chambers. Here he points you to a little stream rushing from amid the rocks and indicates its rise and progress. There he points to some peculiar rock and tells you its name. Then he takes you into a large natural hall and tells you how many persons once feasted in it, and so on.

Truth is a grand series of caverns; it is our glory to have so great and wise a conductor as the Holy Spirit. Imagine that we are coming to the darkness of it. He is a light shining in the midst of us to guide us. And by the light he shows us wondrous things. He teaches us by suggestion, direction, and illumination.

Prayer

LORD God, the Holy Ghost, may faith
grow in men; may they believe in Christ
to the saving of their souls. May their
little faith brighten into strong faith, and
may their strong faith ripen into the full
assurance of faith. May we all have this
last blessing; may we believe God fully;
may we never waver. Resting in the Great
Surety and High Priest of the New Covenant may we feel "the peace of God
which passeth all understanding," and may
we enter into rest. Amen.

Try, For Nothing Is Impossible

48 And Jesus said unto him, No man, having put his hand to the plough, and looking back, is fit for the kingdom of God. — *Luke 9:62*

NO man is likely to accomplish much who moodily indulges a desponding view of his own capacities. By God's help the weakest of us may be strong, and it is the way to become so, to resolve never to give up a good work till we have tried our best to achieve it. To think nothing impossible is the privilege of faith.

We deprecate the indolent cowardice of the man who always felt assured that every new enterprise would be too much for him, and therefore declined it. But we admire the pluck of the ploughman who was asked on his cross-examination if he could read Greek, and replied he did not know, because he had never tried. Those Suffolk horses which will pull at a post till they drop are worth a thousand times as much as jibbing animals that run back as soon as ever the collar begins to press them.

Prayer

LORD, bless the work of the church and all its branches; and let Thy kingdom come into the hearts of multitudes by its means. Remember all churches that are really at work for Jesus, and all private individuals, workers alone, workers by themselves. Amen.

Christian Zeal

49

Fight the good fight of faith, lay hold on eternal life, whereunto thou art also called, and hast professed a good profession before many witnesses. — *I Timothy 6:12*

WHEN the Spartans marched into battle they advanced with cheerful songs, willing to fight. But when the Persians entered the conflict, you could hear, as the regiments came on, the crack of whips by which the officers drove the cowards into the thick of the battle. You need not wonder that a few Spartans were more than a match for thousands of Persians, that in fact they were like lions in the midst of sheep.

So let it be with the church; never should she need to be forced to reluctant action. Full of irrepressible life, she should long for conflict against everything which is contrary to God. Were we enthusiastic soldiers of the cross we should be like lions in the midst of herds of enemies, and through God's help nothing would be able to stand against us.

Prayer

LORD, help us to live such lives as pardoned men should live. We have but a little time to tarry here, for our life is but a vapor; soon it vanishes away. But we are most anxious that we may spend the time here in holy fear and in the Christian fight, that grace may be upon us from the commencement of our Christian life even to the earthly close of it. Amen.

Our Greatest Enemy

50

The heart is deceitful above all things, and desperately wicked: who can know it? I the Lord search the heart, I try the reins, even to give every man according to his ways, and according to the fruit of his doings. — Jeremiah 17:9-10

A GARRISON is not free from danger while it hath an enemy lodged within."

You may bolt all your doors, and fasten all your windows, but if the thieves have placed even a little child within doors, who can draw the bolts for them, the house is still unprotected. All the sea outside a ship cannot do it damage till the water enters within and fills the hold. Hence, it is clear, our greatest danger is from within. All the devils in hell and tempters on earth could do us no injury if there were no corruption in our nature. The sparks will fall harmlessly if there is no tinder. Alas, our heart is our greatest enemy; this is the little home-born thief.

Prayer

LORD, save the careless; save the sinful;
the drunkard, take away from him his cup.
The unholy and unjust men, deliver these
from their filthiness. The dishonest and
false, renew them in their living. Any that
are lovers of self, whose life is bounded
by the narrowness of their own being, the
Lord regenerate and make them new
creatures in Christ Jesus. And cleanse our
own hearts. Amen.

The Full Consequences of Sin

51

Keeping mercy for thousands, forgiving iniquity and transgression and sin, and that will by no means clear the guilty; visiting the iniquity of the fathers upon the children, and upon the children's children, unto the third and to the fourth generation. — Exodus 34:7

SAGES of old contended that no sin was ever committed whose consequences rested on the head of the sinner alone; that no man could do ill and his fellows not suffer. They illustrated it thus: "A vessel sailing from Joppa, carried a passenger, who, beneath his berth, cut a hole through the ship's side. When the men of the watch expostulated with him, 'What doest thou, O miserable man?' the offender calmly replied, 'What matters it to you? The hole I have made lies under my own berth.'"

This ancient parable is worthy of the utmost consideration. No man perishes alone in his iniquity. No man can guess the full consequences of his transgressions.

Prayer

OH! keep us from sin; keep us much in prayer; keep us with the light of God shining on our forehead. May we be a happy people, not because screened from affliction, but because we are walking in the light of God. Amen.

Hitherto

52

Then Samuel took a stone, and set it between Mizpeh and Shen, and called the name of it Ebenezer, saying, Hitherto hath the Lord helped us. — *I Samuel 7:12*

THE word "hitherto" seems like a hand pointing in the direction of the **past.** Twenty years or seventy, and yet "hitherto hath the Lord helped us!" Through poverty, through wealth; through sickness, through health; in perplexity, in joy — "hitherto hath the Lord helped!"

We delight to look down a long avenue of trees. It is delightful to gaze from one end of the long vista, a sort of verdant temple, with its branching pillars and its arches of leaves. Even so look down the long aisles of your years, at the green boughs of mercy overhead, and the strong pillars of lovingkindness and faithfulness which bear up your joys.

Are there no birds in yonder branches singing? Surely there must be many, and they all sing of mercy received "hitherto."

But the word also points **forward.** For when a man gets up to a certain mark and writes "hitherto," he is not yet at the end. There are still distances to be traversed. More trials, more joys; more temptations, more triumphs; more battles, more victories; and then come sickness, disease, death. But when read in Heaven's light, how glorious and marvelous a prospect will thy "hitherto" unfold to thy grateful eye.

Prayer

LORD, we would take afresh the cup of salvation and call upon the name of the Lord. We bless Him who hath redeemed us unto Himself, not with corruptible things as silver and gold, but with His own precious blood; and we do avow ourselves today to be the Lord's. Amen.